NATIONAL
GEOGRA

T0069856

Hands at Work

Freya Purdey

People use their hands at work.

Who is at work?

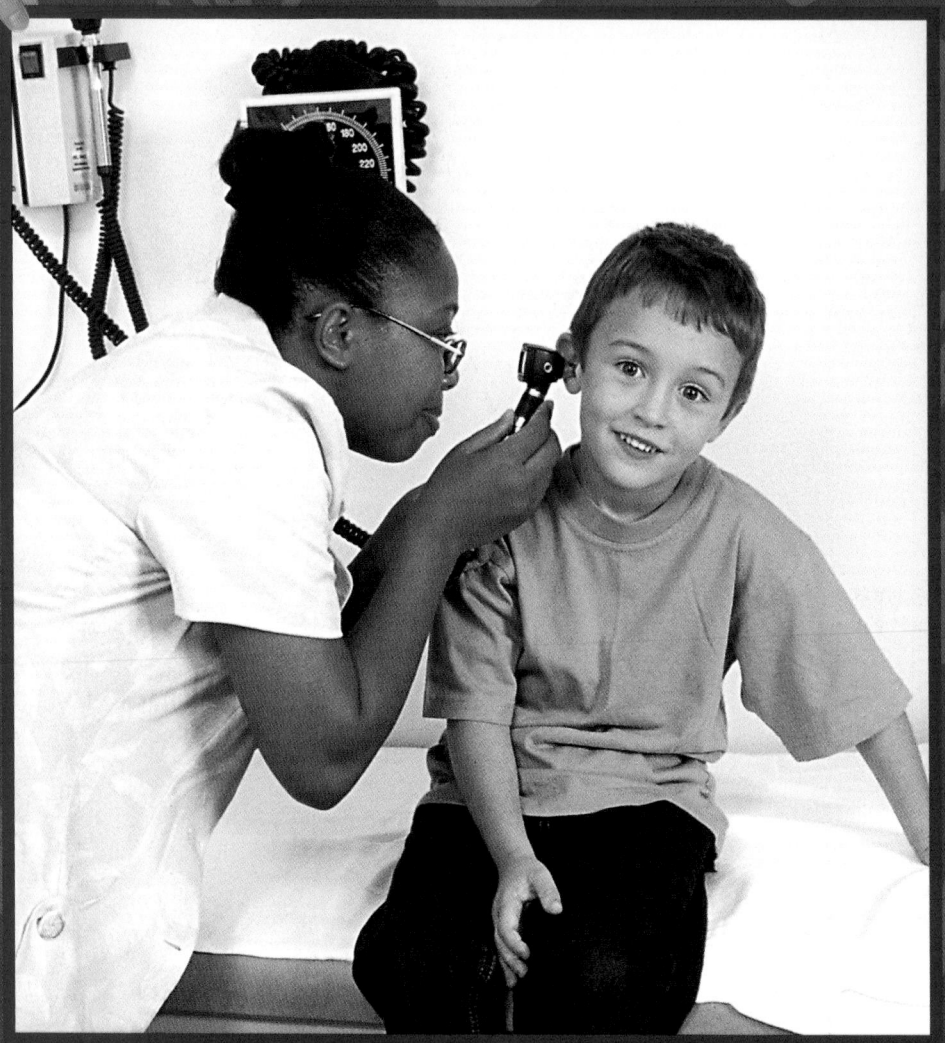

The doctor is at work.

Who is at work?

The gardener is at work.

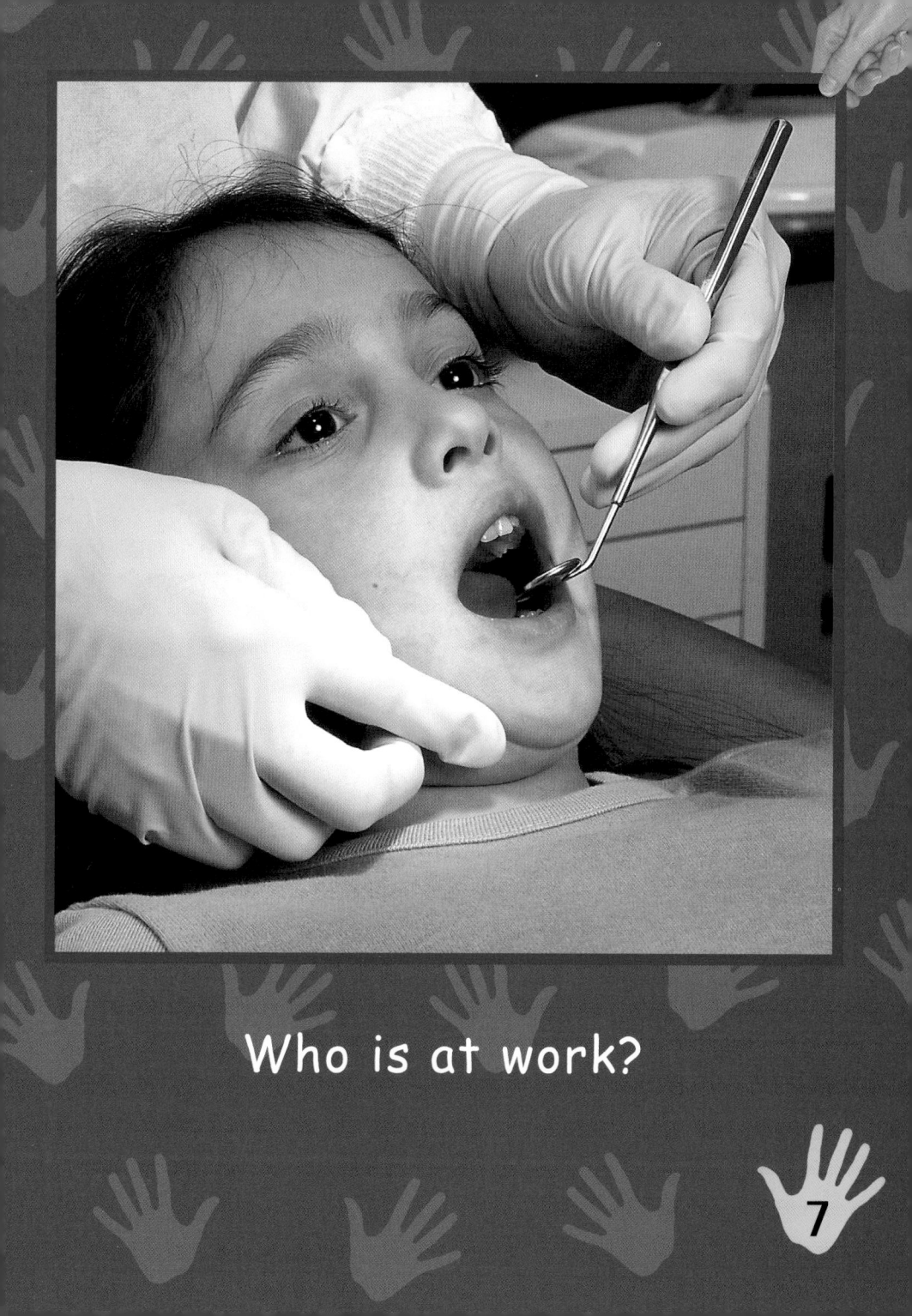

Who is at work?

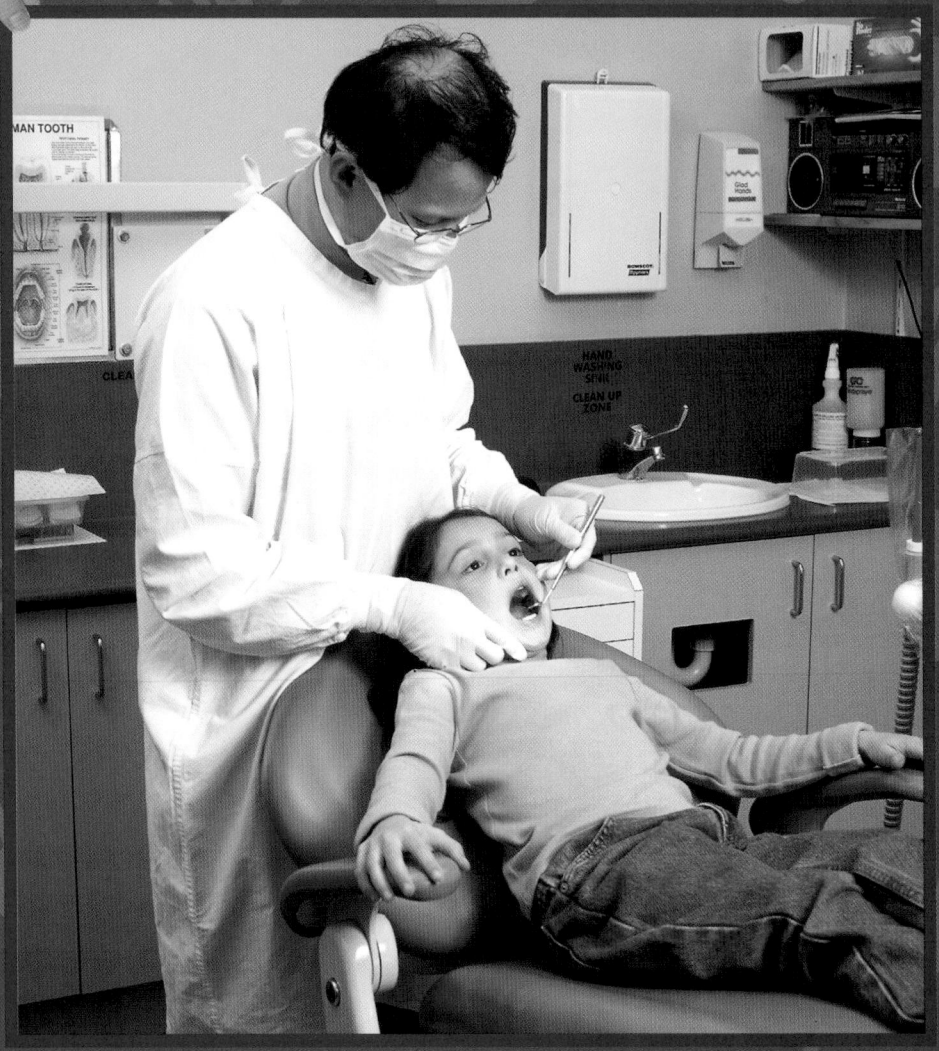

The dentist is at work.

Who is at work?

The carpenter is at work.

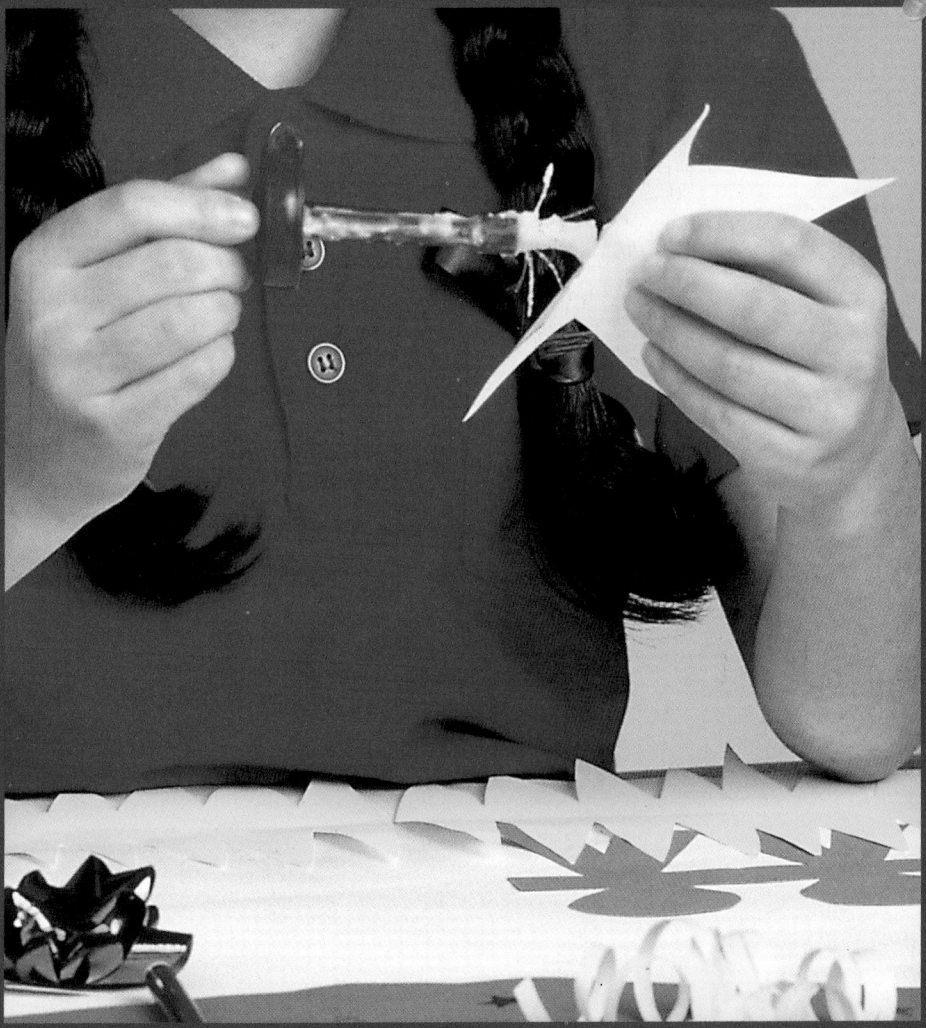

Who is at work?

I am at work.